Chapter 1 – Grounded

Chapter 2 - Rated PG

Chapter 3 – A Bumpy Ride

Chapter 4 – Independence

Chapter 5 – The Game of Life

Chapter 6 – Eyes Wide Open

Chapter 7 – Best Friend Qualities

Chapter 8 – On Your Mark, Get Set, Be Still

Chapter 9 – Got Roots?

Chapter 10 – Consequences

Chapter 11 – Liar, Liar

Chapter 12 – Time to Fly

Chapter 13 – Random Kindness

Chapter 14 – Five More Minutes

Chapter 15 – A New Normal

Chapter 16 – Party Time

Chapter 17 – A Time to Dance

Chapter 18 – Rest Assured

Chapter 19 – Dirty Dishes

Chapter 20 – Run and Not Grow Weary

Chapter 21 – Maybe She's Born with It?

Chapter 22 – Avoid Big Fish

Chapter 23 – Scar

Chapter 24 – We are Rich!

For my son Will

Photography Credit – Jennifer Marie Photography

Ecclesiastes 3: 1-8

There is a time for everything, and a season for every activity under the heavens: a time to be born and a time to die, a time to plant and a time to uproot, a time to kill and a time to heal, a time to tear down and a time to build, a time to weep and a time to laugh, a time to mourn and a time to dance, a time to scatter stones and a time to gather them, a time to embrace and a time to refrain from embracing, a time to search and a time to give up, a time to keep and a time to throw away, a time to tear and a time to mend, a time to be silent and a time to speak, a time to love and a time to hate, a time for war and a time for peace.

CHAPTER 1 – GROUNDED

Will: "Mom what does it mean to get grounded?"

Mom: "That for a set period of time you lose the privilege of doing something you like to do."

Will: "Who decides the grounding?"

Mom: "I do! Is there something you want to tell me?"

Will: "No. I'm just planning ahead."

According to Wikipedia, an anchor is "a device, normally made of metal, used to connect a vessel to the bed of a body of water to prevent the craft from drifting due to wind or current. The word derives from Latin *ancora,* which itself comes from the Greek ἄγκυρα *(ankura).* Anchors can either be temporary or permanent." A device that prevents a craft from drifting. I wonder what helps you when you start to drift. What anchors you?

What intrigues me most about the process of lowering an anchor is that for an anchor to find a strong foothold it first needs to sink. The anchor needs to head deeper and deeper into the depths of the water. The anchor passes through the sun-splintered surface and travels to where light becomes swallowed up by darkness. The water temperature becomes colder and colder, the surroundings are unfamiliar, and visibility becomes cloudy, yet the anchor continues to plummet. Sinking lower and lower, it moves away from the surface and out of sight. Finally, the anchor connects with the solid ground and digs in.

When I think about the most difficult and painful moments of my life, I can relate to a sinking anchor. Sinking was exactly the feeling I was experiencing. I felt cold, overwhelmed by my situation, and enveloped by the darkness that surrounded me. I was fearful of the shadows lurking in the unfamiliar waters and longed for the warm, calm surface. I was afraid that the farther I traveled the less "anchored" I would be, and what would await me when I finally hit the bottom?

This world offers all sorts of temporary anchors for us. But what happens when we start to drift and face those rough seas? The loss of a job, a loved one, a dream? When we toss our anchor over the side of our chaotic life, are we casting it out of desperation or are we hopeful that it will find a strong foothold?

Whether you are mindlessly drifting in calm seas or being tossed about by rough waves, I pray that you reach out to the ONE who can calm the seas with just His voice. The One who can provide a permanent anchor to anyone whose soul is sinking.

Hebrews 6:19

"We have this hope as an anchor for the soul, firm and secure."

CHAPTER 2 – RATED PG

Mom: "Would you like to help me with a job or read?"

Will: "Well Mom, that's a tough choice. If I read for 20 minutes that would make me smarter but if I help you vacuum that teaches me responsibility."

What do you think of when you see the acronym PG? The Motion Picture Association of America (MPAA) uses PG on their film rating system for films where "some material may not be suitable for children. May contain some material parents might not like for their young children." As parents we have a responsibility to shield our children from inappropriate subject matter and to help expose them to material that helps their hearts and minds to mature in a healthy way.

Recently I have had the opportunity to spend some time with my 84-year-old father as he recovers from heart surgery. My dad was born in 1934, served in the army, and graduated from Michigan State University with honors. He remembers hearing the news of Pearl Harbor on the radio, where he was when John F. Kennedy was assassinated and when man first walked on the moon. He has calloused hands, deep wrinkles from sun exposure and blue eyes that still twinkle when he tells a favorite story. Every night at 7:30 he enjoys two guilty pleasures: a bowl of strawberry ice cream and watching Jeopardy.

Since my dad's surgery, 5 bypasses and a heart valve replacement, I have witnessed a frailty in him that I had not noticed before. Just last summer my dad was still driving his tractor up and down fields he has managed his entire life and tossing bales of hay around like they were piles of leaves. These days my dad's jeans hang loosely around his waist due to loss of appetite, and his calloused hands are riddled with arthritis. He needs a little extra help when buttoning his shirt and climbing the stairs. The spring in his step is still there, but the spring has lost some of its bounce.

As we age, we tend to look back on our lives and reminisce about memories like scenes from a movie. There are moments of sheer joy, moments of deep pain and lots of little moments in between. There are some memories that we could watch repeatedly and others we cannot believe that we survived them.

In this age of technology, we have more opportunities to capture videos our lives and I often find myself watching videos from my son's early years. I see him struggle to button up his coat, his curiosity driving him to explore everything around him and me offering to help him when he needed it. These days my son needs less of my assistance; so now that same assistance has been re-directed to my father. I want my son to see how parental guidance is still needed whether you are the parent or the child. Compassion for those you love is hopefully something you never grow out of and is something you will need whether you are four or eighty-four.

It has been said that at the end of our life we will see scenes of our lives. I am sure there will be moments of disappointment where I could have done more or made better choices. Hopefully, there will be moments when God's plan for my life and my actions were more in sync than not. And I sure hope there is popcorn.

Psalm 71:9

"Do not cast me off in the time of old age; forsake me when my strength is spent.

CHAPTER 3 – A BUMPY RICH

Will: "Mom when is Jesus coming back?"

Mom: "I don't know, pal."

Will: "Sometimes I wish we could start this whole thing all over."

If you have ever flown on a commercial aircraft, you are probably familiar with the announcement that takes place right before the plane is ready for take-off.

"Ladies and gentlemen, the captain has turned on the fasten seat belt sign. Please stow your carry-on luggage underneath the seat in front of you or in an overhead bin. Please take your seat, fasten your seat belt, and make sure your seat back and folding trays are in their full upright position."

Recently I was on a flight, bound for vacation, and it was a beautiful day for flying. We were cruising at a comfortable thirty-six thousand feet and I was blissfully relaxed as I thought about the vacation days that lay before me. I love that feeling of shedding my mom cloak of responsibilities and slipping on my explorer outfit, complete with passport, journal, and a camera. Over the airplane's speaker system, the captain announced that we should take our seats and fasten our seat belts because there was turbulence ahead. As I looked out my small window, all I could see was clear blue skies and white puffy clouds. Then it occurred to me that the captain had a much bigger view of what was ahead than I did. What did he see that prompted a warning about buckling our seat belts? Do we ever get warnings like that in day-to-day life? How can we be prepared when turbulence appears on the horizon?

Thankfully, we have a God that is the most capable pilot. He sees every minute of our lives and knows the pains, heartaches and joy that will fill our days on this earth. He is always waiting to assure us that no matter how bumpy the ride gets, how taxing the delays become, or how frustrating the missed connections are, He will be there. He even warns us of difficult times ahead in *John 16:33*: *"I have told you these things, so that in me you may have peace. In this world you will have trouble. But take heart! I have overcome the world."* If I just focus on the part that tells me I will have trouble I start to worry and get filled with anxiety, waiting for that trouble to appear. However, if I shift my focus to the promise that comes before the warning, my fear dissolves. God wants us to have peace…a peace that is found only in Him. That is a promise I can bet my life on.

The next time you are experiencing a turbulent situation, take a deep breath, trust your pilot, and buckle up.

Psalm 139:9-10

"If I rise on the wings of the dawn, if I settle on the far side of the sea, even there

your hand will guide me, your right hand will hold me fast.

CHAPTER 4 - INDEPENDENCE

Will: "Hey mom, I think I just need your help to drive our car and get my breakfast, but I can do everything else, okay?"

Mom: "Oh really? Well, that is fabulous. Thank you pal! I will have so much free time on my hands. By the way, you know you do not have pants on, right?"

Will: "Oh yeah...but that's okay."

Independence. What a wonderful part of growing up! We start thinking that we are so ready to face the world and handle any challenges that life has to offer. As a parent it sure is exciting as my son learns to take care of himself and needs less of my "hands-on" help. Of course, the flip side of that is that my little boy needs me less than he used to. That is a bitter pill to swallow. I think the one of the most challenging aspects of parenting has got to be letting our child make their own mistakes and not jump in to fix it. We must step back and let them deal with hurt feelings, disappointments, and consequences.

What do you think of when you hear the word independence? Do images of parades, backyard barbecues and flags waving float through your mind? The Fourth of July is a federal holiday for Americans in which we commemorate the adoption of the Declaration of the Independence. We declared that we were a new nation and no longer under the rule of the British Empire. Such a young country we were, with an unmarked, bright future ahead of us. We have come so far, and yes, we made so many mistakes. Slavery, a civil war between the north and south in which six hundred and twenty thousand loved ones perished, assassinations of leaders, and the list goes on and on. When I think about those blemishes in our nation's history, I feel ashamed, horrified, and hopeless that it will ever get better. Thankfully, there is One that offers grace, forgiveness, and hope, no matter what the sin was.

As I watched my son grow, I have seen him make many mistakes: say words he regretted later, suffer tough consequences due to inappropriate behavior and choices that in hindsight were regretful. In each one of those situations there were tears, tough conversations, and accountability, but those are things we all experience at some point in our lives. A loving parent knows that they need to discipline a beloved child, because it is so important to that child's growth and development. Just like our Heavenly Father does for His beloved children.

Our Heavenly Father allows us to have independence to make our own decisions and our own mistakes. He offers guidance through His Word, giving us friends whose counsels gives us accountability and many opportunities to make choices out of love instead of selfish gain. What a great example of parenting to follow!

I hope that you take time to celebrate your personal independence from sin, and as you continue to mature that your opportunities to show God's love light up the sky!

Romans 8:21

"That the creation itself will be set free from its bondage to corruption and obtain the freedom of the glory of the children of God.

CHAPTER 5 – THE GAME OF LIFE

Will: "Mom listen. So first you go to school, then you got to work and then you get old? That is NOT a good plan."

Recently my son has become fascinated with The Game of Life. Have you ever played that board game? It is a fantastic game that gives each player the opportunity to make life decisions such as pursuing a career, going to college, getting married, having children, and deciding on whether to purchase a home. We have spent hours playing this game, giving silly nicknames to our fictitious spouses and children, who are symbolized as little blue and pink pegs inserted in our plastic vehicles. Good times indeed! If you do not have it, I encourage you to add it to your board game collection.

When I was pregnant, I made the mistake of reading the book that every pregnant mother receives: What to Expect When You Are Expecting. If you happen to be pregnant right now, do yourself a favor. Put that book down and learn something useful, like knitting. Trust me. Trying to create something using two sharp needles will be far easier than trying to do everything in that book. After reading the first few chapters, I felt completely unequipped to become a mother. I knew right then, before I even saw my son's face, that I was going to make mistakes and that there would be times when he did not like me and vice versa. I was not going to be the mom that made fabulous home-made dinners from scratch or that grew her own vegetables. I was not going to be that mom who designed amazing Halloween costumes or volunteered for every school event. But what kind of mom did I did want to be? I thought about what I had learned in the thirty plus years I had been alive and what values I wanted my son to learn about. I knew I could not do everything well, but I could certainly focus on a few things and do those to the best of my ability.

I want my son to have a love of reading. Not only the ability TO read, (add comma) but a lifelong craving to pick up a book and devour ever word, using his imagination to make the characters come alive. I began to read to my son when he was still in the womb. Every night when I would read to him, he would cease his constant rib kicking (a soccer player already?) and become very still, almost as if he were already listening to the stories he was hearing. Years later and reading before bedtime is still a part of our daily routine. I can still remember the night he turned the page for the first time and when he read an entire book by himself. Gone are the days he would curl up in my lap, but the love of reading is still there. I hope reading is a habit he continues for years to come. All the while the wheel in Game of Life keeps spinning.

I want my son to have a passion for adventure. I want him to put aside the day-to-day routines of his life and take off to distant lands, meet new people and explore the sights and sounds of the new surroundings. I hope a camera, a travel journal, and his passport are things that get used repeatedly with or without someone to travel with. I hope he finds the time to head off on a long road trip or backpack through a foreign country. All the while the wheel in Game of Life keeps spinning.

Most importantly I want my son to have a belief in God. A strong faith in the unseen continuous working of a higher power. At the beginning of every school year, I give my son a bible verse that he must recite before getting out of the car to start his school day. At dinner, every night we each write down one thing we are grateful for, and at night the last word he says before drifting off to sleep is "amen," signifying his personal prayer is done. I hope that faith stays with him long after my days have ended. All the while the wheel in Game of Life keeps spinning.

As I listen to my son talk about his future and share in the excitement of those dreams, I quickly get overwhelmed thinking of all the things I still have left to teach him and how eighteen years will not be enough time. We still need to focus on skills such as time management, financial responsibility, the value of hard work, plus the basics of learning to do his own laundry, and how to cook. I know our nights of sharing dinner around the table and playing board games will become few and far between as his life gets busier. But for now, I will continue to enjoy every spin of the wheel in The Game of Life.

Psalm 32:8

"I will instruct you and teach you in the way you should go; I will counsel you with my loving eye on you."

CHAPTER 6 – EYES WIDE OPEN

Mom: "Hey little boy, you need to close those blue eyes now."

Will: "But then I won't be able to see how much I love you."

A few weeks ago, I misplaced my sunglasses at a time when I desperately needed them. The chilly and rainy day had suddenly taken a turn for the better and sunshine was beginning to peek through the clouds. If you live in Michigan, you will completely understand that drastic change in weather. My son and I were headed out of town to visit my dad for Father's Day and I knew I would need my sunglasses for the long drive north. I looked in the car, under the seat, and in my bag but I could not find them anywhere, and my back-up pair was missing as well. What a day.

Ever have one of those?

Different eyewear provides our eyes with the ability to have clearer vision, puts objects into focus and protects our eyes. Sunglasses are used to protect our eyes from the ultraviolet rays of the sun. Contact lenses and eyeglasses are used to correct vision deficiencies and improve our vision. Goggles allow us to see under water and safety glasses protect our eyes from harmful environments. Of course, if you are like me and have reached the age when reading glasses are required, then that just adds a whole new vision dynamic.

I wonder if our eyes need protection from more than we think. Do we need spiritual eye protection or vision correction?

There are several times in the scriptures when it talks about people's eyes being opened. The phrase "to open someone's eyes" means to "enlighten someone about certain realities and/or to cause someone to realize or discover something." After Adam and Eve sinned, their "*eyes were opened*" to the fact that they were naked, and that sin was present. In Psalms 119:18 we read, *"Open my eyes to see the wonderful truths in your instructions."* Matthew 6:22-23 tells us that our eyes are the lamp of our body. *"The eye is the lamp of the body. So, if your eye is healthy, your whole body will be full of light, but if your eye is bad, your whole body will be full of darkness. If then the light in you is darkness, how great is the darkness!"*

Our sinful nature wants us to focus only on ourselves, our needs, wants and desires. We want eyewear that protects our eyes from the blinding glare of honesty, integrity, and accountability. However, God was us to open our eyes to His truth, His Love and His Grace so that we no longer must walk in darkness. He is the Son that sheds light into the darkest places and gives our eyes the protection they need when the sinfulness of this world threatens to blind us.

So how do we improve our spiritual vision? The first step could be turning our eyes away from social media that distracts us from our walk with God. Or maybe it is deciding that instead of playing another level of Candy Crush we let our eyes become focused on a weekly bible verse. It could be as simple as praying that God opens your eyes to those in need around you. Whatever it is I pray that Clara H. Scott's words inspire you to obtain 20/20 vision.

Open my eyes, that I may see
Glimpses of truth Thou hast for me;
Place in my hands the wonderful key
That shall unclasp and set me free.

Open My Eyes, That I May See – Clara H. Scott

Ephesians 1:18

"I pray that the eyes of your heart may be enlightened in order that you may know the hope to which he has called

you, the riches of his glorious inheritance in his holy people."

CHAPTER 7 – BEST FRIEND QUALITIES

Joanne: "What do you like about your best friend?"

Will: "He's calm and steady and he laughs at my jokes."

When you think of your best friend(s), what comes to mind? What qualities do they possess that you admire and value as part of their friendship? Maybe they are the 'life of the party' and every time you get together a memorable experience splashes all over your social media. Maybe they are the voice of reason when you are having one of those indecisive life moments that leaves you uncertain as to which path to take. Whatever those qualities are that your best friend(s), possesses it is likely their friendship positively impacts your life and hopefully you are a better person for it.

Every day after school I ask my son specific questions about his day. What did he have for lunch, what did he do at recess and who did he play with? During these elementary years I typically hear him mention the same names repeatedly, describing those friends as his best friends. After multiple play dates with the same friend, I asked my son what he likes so much about that friend. As usual his response was priceless. He described his friend as calm, steady and someone who laughs as his jokes. Is that how you would describe your best friend(s)? When I think of the friends who make up my inner circle, I would use those exact words. What words would my friends use when describing me?

When I think of the darkest times in my life, I think of the friends who were there for me. I do not remember all their comforting words, but I remember their faces. The friend who showed up to help me pick out clothes for my mother's funeral. The friend who just stopped by, knowing how lonely I can get when my son is visiting his dad for the weekend. The friend who continually asks me how they can pray for me. Having another friend walking beside me, whether physically or through prayers, always seems to be the right amount of comfort and a wonderful reminder that I am not alone. Even God understood loneliness when He said that His greatest masterpiece of creation, Adam, was alone so He created another human being.

According to Merriam Webster, a friend is described as "a favored companion." I know I have been blessed to have several amazing friends who hold me accountable, who challenge me to be more, who encourage me, and pray for me. As I thought about friendship, I was reminded of a song from Sunday School that I learned as a child.

What a friend we have in Jesus

all our sins and griefs to bear
What a privilege to carry

everything to God in prayer
Oh, what peace we often forfeit

Oh, what needless pain we bear
All because we do not carry

Everything to God in prayer
Have we trials and temptations

Is there trouble anywhere
We should never be discouraged

Take it to the Lord in prayer

Can we find a friend so faithful
Who will all our sorrows share?
Jesus knows our every weakness
Take it to the Lord in prayer

Songwriters: Charles Crozat Converse / Joseph Scriven

Proverbs 27:9

"A sweet friend refreshes the soul."

CHAPTER 8 – ON YOUR MARK, GET SET, BE STILL

Will: "Mom, when your brain gets tired of thinking, daydreaming takes over and that's when the trouble starts."

What do you miss most about childhood? As a kid I loved swinging on the swing set at school and gazing up at the blue sky with those enormous white puffy clouds. I innocently thought if I just pumped my legs hard enough, I would be able to jump off my swing and land on one of those clouds, which would envelop me like a giant pillow. I could spend hours thinking about life and dreaming about the future. I would imagine what I would look like in the years to come, places I would travel to, and all the new friends I would meet. What I liked most about daydreaming is that it requires you to be still. Your body cannot be in motion nor can you be busy doing something else like cooking, doing laundry or balancing a spreadsheet to give daydreaming your full intention.

As an adult there just does not seem to be any time to enjoy the simple pleasure of daydreaming or even time to take a few minutes to just be still. These days I must intentionally schedule time to be still by putting a reminder on my phone to make it a priority. As a parent, I cannot even use the peace and quiet of a bathroom break without my son picking that exact moment to tell me something that just cannot wait five minutes. When I was pregnant, I began the practice of yoga and nine years later I still cannot wait to put my bare feet on my mat, I know that for the next hour I just get to breathe and stretch. In my opinion, yoga is less about twisting myself in knots; instead, it is about learning how to breathe. Deep breathing. Breathing in life and breathing out the things that have caused me anxiety or worry. At the beginning of each class, the instructor would ask "what is your intention" for this practice and ask us to focus on that as we move through the practice. For the first five minutes I would struggle to shut off the mental lists that were flying through my mind: groceries that I needed to pick up and chores that needed to be completed. Every time that I would let those thoughts take over, I would inevitably lose my balance and had to begin again. With practice the focus, breathing and yoga have gotten easier. I guess that is why yoga is called a practice. Maybe that is how I should approach life by asking myself daily what is my intention? Or better yet, what is God's intention for me?

Maybe being still is easy for you, but for most of us I bet it is a work-out. Thankfully, it is not the type of workout that requires special clothing, equipment, or a gym membership but it is certainly a lot harder that I thought it would be. After a church retreat a few years ago, I decided that solitude time would be my spiritual discipline and what a discipline it has been. During that period of my life, I was an emotional wreck, and I would spend my dedicated solitude time just crying. I would set the timer on my phone for just ten minutes with the intention of achieving mindfulness, and after thirty seconds I would be a blubbering mess. I would let the tears stream down my face, surrounded by a pile of wrinkled, wet tissues all the while my body began to melt with release of all that pent-up sorrow. When the timer went off, I felt exhausted but peaceful. Thankfully, over time, that practice of stillness has gotten easier and so has the deep breathing. Breath is life and it was the breath of God that gave life to man.

Genesis 2:7 "Then the LORD God formed a man from the dust of the ground and breathed into his nostrils the breath of life, and the man became a living being."

These days I still set my timer for ten minutes, with tissues within reach. I find more strength in being still for those precious ten minutes than I ever did running a ½ marathon. Maybe it is the power of prayer, the miracle of mindfulness or stability in stillness, but each minute gives me clarity, strength, and peace of mind. Maybe day dreaming is just the beginning step towards mindfulness?

Exodus 14:14

"The Lord will fight for you while you keep still."

CHAPTER 9 – GOT ROOTS?

Will: "Why is lightning loud?"

Joanne: "I think it is because it has lots of energy. Why do you think it is loud?"

Will: "I think because God is frustrated, and He just needs to get it out!"

I grew up on a farm that has been in our family for over 150 years. My summer breaks from school involved exciting opportunities like picking asparagus, planting crops, driving tractors and my personal favorite, baling hay. Our home was surrounded with crop fields and acres of woods. I remember countless hayrides through those woods, endless days constructing forts and tapping trees for maple syrup. I loved walking through those woods and marveling at the tall trees that stretch their long limbs up to the sunlight. I loved the shaded canopy they provided and the mossy ground that lay at their feet, wondering what the trees would say if they could talk. What stories would they tell in the hundreds of years they had spent there?

Occasionally I would come across a tree that had fallen to the ground, with its tangled roots exposed, and I would be overcome with sadness. What type of storm had the power to rip that mighty wood giant from its deeply rooted foothold and toss it aside like it was a twig? How long had the tree swayed back and forth, thrashing at the wind and rain until it realized it was powerless and it finally gave up? How long would it lay there, no longer able to feel the sun on its shoulders or the soft breezes blowing through its leaves? I would lay my hand on the tree, feeling the rough bark under my fingers and study the lines that are engraved on its trunk, marking the passage of time like the wrinkles that show up on our own faces as we age. I prefer to refer to them as laugh lines, but some of those wrinkles are from moments that caused me great joy, but others are the result of deep pain.

What piqued my interest the most about a fallen tree was what lay at its base. Prior to the powerful storm, that mighty tree had stood tall and proud, a majestic sight to behold. It showed no sights of weakness, no internal struggles or rotted out core. But after the storm, that tree lay toppled over, vulnerable, and exposed. You could see exactly what had held that tree up and how vulnerable it was to being pushed over. Sometimes I would find trees that were as strong on the inside as they appeared on the outside. Their trunks were composed of layer upon layer of life that showed they had been through seasons of plenty and want, surplus and famine, always reaching upward towards the sun. On other occasions I would discover trees with hollowed out cores and rotted root systems. It was no surprise that they now lay on the ground because they had no foothold and no inner strength to draw from when the storms came.

According to the Word of God, every single person will experience troubles in this life. Sometimes I even question whether some people have been dealt more than their fair share. Yet those people are exactly the ones who set the bar for how to push ahead even during the greatest grief and disappointment. I would bet that if you take the opportunity to hear their stories you would find out that their core is lined with a belief in something greater than themselves, and their root system is filled with soul-quenching nutrients. What if we behaved more like trees? Anchoring ourselves deeply in the Word of God and reaching upwards toward the Son so that we can reach out to those in need, provide shade to those seeking comfort and support those in search of a place to rest. What a beautiful forest THAT would be, filled with trees that are rooted in faith, and one that I would love to walk through and be a part of.

Jeremiah 17:7-8

"Blessed is the man who trusts in the Lord, whose trust is the Lord. He is like a tree planted by water, that sends out its roots by the stream, and does not fear when heat comes, for its leaves remain green, and is not anxious in the year of drought, for it does not cease to bear fruit."

CHAPTER 10 - CONSEQUENCES

Will: "Mom, here is what I think my consequence should be."

Joanne: "Consequence? For what?"

Will: "I don't think that's important."

You know it is going to be a long school year when your first grader throws out a word like 'consequence' during the first week of school. Then you must deal with the fallout when you gently inform him that he does not get to choose his consequence.

Consequences are such a pain, aren't they? A consequence is defined as result or effect of our actions. It sure would be nice if we got to choose the consequences. I bet they would be a lot less painful and heartbreaking if we did. What is the most painful consequence you have experienced? I can admit that I have made some poor choices in the relationship arena and those have consistently brought devastating consequences. Rejection, loneliness, and a broken heart, and yet God has used every one of those consequences to create a work of art.

In the Bible there are two women, who shared similar stories of rejection and brokenness, yet their lives had a significant and positive impact on God's story. I am sure they did not go to sleep every night thinking how satisfying and fulfilled their lives were, but rather how lonely and disappointing, and that is something to which I can relate.

In the Old Testament there was a woman named Hagar, who was an Egyptian slave. Her female mistress was unable to bear children, so she used Hagar, forcing Hagar to sleep with her husband and Hagar became pregnant. I am sure that was not in Hagar's original job description and yet she was obedient. Then another ugly vice, jealousy, appeared and drove the mistress to mistreat Hagar to the point where Hagar ran away. Can you imagine the negative thoughts running through Hagar's head as she ran away? "How could I be so stupid? I thought my mistress loved me. I feel so used! Now I am pregnant, on my own, and have no idea how I am going to survive, let alone take care of a baby." Any of those thoughts seem familiar? Yet even in her darkest hour, an angel appeared to her, reassured her that God had heard her prayer. God would "increase (her)your descendants so much that they will be too numerous to count." Our God is a God who hears our pleas and issues a blessing. That is my kind of God.

Another woman featured in the Old Testament is Rahab, a prostitute living in the city of Jericho. I do not know if you can get much lower in the socio-economic class than a prostitute.
A woman who survived by trading her body for any means necessary. I bet she did not dream of that career choice when she was a little girl. Every knock at her door was most likely another 'customer' and meant her self-worth was going to take another blow. One night there came a different knock at her door and two strangers appeared, and they needed a place to hide. These men were spies from a neighboring country who were planning an attack on Jericho. That attack that would burn the entire city to the ground, leaving no one alive except an obedient prostitute and her entire family.   Our God is a God who opens our doors to salvation. That is my kind of God.

One of my favorite types of art is mosaics. An artist takes broken pieces of materials, such as glass, tile, shells, placing each one in just the right spot to create a beautiful piece of artwork. I can stare at a mosaic for hours, admiring the painstaking and time-consuming dedication it requires of the artist. It takes the eyes of a gifted artist to look at broken pieces of glass, something that most people would discard or throw away, and use each one of them to create a masterpiece. Each piece is handled with care and all the past grime is washed away. Through the eyes of the artist, each piece is gazed upon as the perfect addition. It is just the right shape, the right color, and its brokenness is what makes it so invaluable. Our God is a God who uses the broken and the discarded to create mosaics. My kind of art, my kind of masterpiece and my kind of God

Jeremiah 17:14

"God, pick up the pieces. Put me back together again.

CHAPTER 11 – LIAR, LIAR

Will: "Mom, do you want to know what reverse psychology is?"

Joanne: "Yes I would love to know that."

Will "It is when you say the opposite of what you want your kid to do. Like if you want them to turn the TV off you tell them I sure hope you do not turn that TV off."

With a child in elementary school, I am constantly reminded of those little schoolyard rhymes and taunts that never seem to go out of style. Do you remember those? "Sticks and stones can break you bones but words will never hurt you?" I have found that there is a lot of power in words, and when words are used as weapons, they can leave deep wounds. Another schoolyard taunt one that seems to have stood the test of time is "liar, liar, pants on fire, hanging from a telephone wire." I would suspect that if a person's pants caught fire immediately upon verbalizing a lie, we would all be a bit kinder, smarter, and need a lot more fire extinguishers. What motivates someone to tell a lie and perhaps more importantly, what convinces someone to believe a lie? What about the lies we tell ourselves?

I do not know exactly when I started to believe the lies that I began to tell myself. Lies that made me feel that I was not good enough, not smart enough, and not pretty enough. I honestly do not remember anyone ever saying those words directly to me, yet somehow, they became part of my internal belief system. Over time I began to believe those lies and trust them as truth. Then when something as insignificant as not being invited to a party or not attaching a file to an email at work occurred, I would let those little lies become my truth. Lies that had no foothold in truth, but I believed them, nonetheless. What are the lies that you tell yourself?

A few years ago, I decided to really pay attention to what I was telling myself and to decide what was true and what was false. Did the number of likes on my social media posts determine that I was worthy of being a friend? Did the fact that I was divorced mean that I was not lovable? The first step in my search for the truth was to determine where I would find it. Thankfully, I did not have to search long because all the answers that I was seeking could be found in scripture. Psalm 33:4 states that "For the word of the Lord is right and true; He is faithful in all He does." The word of the Lord is true. Is it as simple as that? The easy part was accepting that scripture was true, but the hard part was replacing the lies with truth…repeatedly. I believe that any lie that you have chosen to believe about yourself can be erased with the truth that can be found in scripture.

The truth shall set you free and it certainly has set me free. Free from thinking I am not worthy to knowing I am my Savior's masterpiece, fashioned in His image and designed to be His light to a world living in darkness.

John 8:31-32

"So, Jesus said to the Jews who had believed him, "If you abide in my word, you are truly my disciples, and you will know the truth, and the truth will set you free."

CHAPTER 12 - TIME TO FLY

Will: "Mom how hard is the bar exam? I've heard it's pretty hard."

Mom: "The bar exam to become a lawyer? Yes, I believe it's fairly difficult."

Will: "Okay. I'm going to work on that this summer."

Mom: "Excellent. You do know we are going to third grade parent teacher conferences tonight, right?"

Have you ever been afraid of failing? Come on, let me see a raise of hands. In fact, I will raise both hands because I am overtly guilty of that crime. You see I suffer from that harmful vice known as perfectionism. Anne Wilson Schaef, a psychologist and author, once said that "perfectionism is self-abuse of the highest order." Isn't that a mood killer? Trying to be the best, to be perfect, to strive for perfectionism is self-abuse. Yikes!

I think there should be a twelve-step program for people who suffer from this condition. We could all gather in a quiet room, sit on those cold metal chairs that are arranged in a circle and take turns introducing ourselves. "Hello, my name is Joanne. I am a perfectionist. It has been forty days since my last attempt at being perfect." We could mark our success with little tokens and work through the twelve steps of AA. I think I could get through most of those steps quickly until I reached step eight. That is where the rubber would meet the road. Step eight is "make a list of all persons we had harmed and became willing to make amends to them all." (2018 Alcoholics Anonymous Great Britain Ltd). How do you go about making amends with yourself? How would you apologize to yourself for every attempt at trying to be perfect and the times when you didn't even try to do something because you were afraid it would be less than perfect? That is what worries me most about looking this vice in the mirror. Coming face to face with every opportunity where I could have done more, been more, reached for more…but did not because I was afraid of failing. Of being less than perfect. And how do I go about moving forward and not letting that vice hold me back anymore? To try something and being 'okay' when the results are less than perfect? And how do I encourage my son to not make the same mistakes of reaching for the unattainable level of perfectionism? My worst fear would be passing that self-degrading personality struggle down to him.

As part of my recovery, I have decided to stop holding myself back from trying things that I might fail at. During my travels I came across a quote by Erin Hanson that serves as a perfect reminder to me that there are two options at every opportunity that life presents.

"There is freedom waiting for you, on the breezes of the sky,

and you ask, "What if I fall?" Oh, my darling, what if you fly?"

We all afraid of falling. And that fear is so strong that we hold ourselves back and resist taking even one step in the direction you are being called to go. There is also the other possibility of flying. Where we push that fear of failure aside and jump, knowing that no matter what we are giving the opportunity our best.

Something that has been nagging me for about five years now is writing. It began as a quiet voice in my head. What would I write about? Travel, my divorce, my career, none of that seemed noteworthy. So, I made excuses, and more excuses until that nagging, or divine prodding, wore me down. I knew I had to put aside every distraction and perfectionist thought that was preventing me from pursuing this opportunity. At the beginning of the Lenten Season, I decided to take a break from social media. That was one distraction I did not need getting in the way. One morning, I knew what I needed to write about. Ever since then, the words and ideas have come bursting out of my mind like a tidal wave. Believe me, when I say that they are not my words but come from a much greater source. A perfect source. I just needed to put aside some distractions, let go of my perfectionist restrictions, spread my wings…and fly.

Matthew 10:19-20 "Do not worry about what to say or how to say it. At that time, you will be given what to say, for it will not be you speaking, but the Spirit of your Father speaking through you."

CHAPTER 13 – RANDOM KINDNESS

Will: "Mom, I don't always like doing the thing you make me do but I really like the way they make me feel."

Every December a small elf, dressed in red, appears at our house. He is a Christmas Elf and we have named him "Sneaky". Our elf typically brings surprises, likes to play hide, and seek and throughout the Christmas season he challenges a little boy to perform ROK's (also known as random act of kindness). Thank goodness for Pinterest!

This past summer a friend gave me a small book that has deeply impacted my life. So much so that I felt a spiritual nudge to start a small faith-based book club, so I could share that book with others. The book, written by Clare DeGraff, is entitled "The Ten Second Rule: Following Jesus Made Simple". The books message is to do the next thing you are reasonably certain Jesus wants you to do it and do it within the next ten seconds. Seems simple enough. What a great way for Christians to imitate Jesus and how He calls us to demonstrate His greatest command....to love Him and love one another.

Have you ever felt an internal prompt to do something for someone else? Maybe that elderly person needs help pushing their cart back into the store or that young mom juggling three kids needs an extra hand. So why aren't your feet moving or your hands reaching out assist them? It might be uncomfortable, it might take a few minutes longer than you have time to spare, or it might be outside your comfort zone. A random act of kindness should not be all that random lives, should it? They should be something we do without a second thought. What holds us back?

If we were completely honest with ourselves, our number one reason for NOT performing a random act of kindness is selfishness. Maybe we think we do not have the time, the money, or the resources to truly make a difference in another human being's life. How could one small act of kindness make that much difference? Maybe our small-minded perspective and sinful nature get in the way. If we say we are Christians who believe in one almighty God, a God who holds eternity in His hands, how can we possibly think that opportunities for random acts of kindness are random? What if they are moments that were ordained long before we took our first step? If we claim to worship a God who knows the numbers of hairs on our heads, designed us in our mother's womb and paid for our sins long before we committed them, then isn't it likely that same God has orchestrated moments for us to show His love and show our obedience?

Romans 7:21-23 "So I find this law at work: Although I want to do good, evil is right there with me. For in my inner being I delight in God's law; but I see another law at work in me, waging war against the law of my mind and making me a prisoner of the law of sin at work within me."

One of my son's ROK's last year was to present a coffee gift card to a stranger. According to my young son there is nothing less exciting than walking up to a stranger. However, the surprised look on that stranger's face was pure joy! The afterglow of warmth that spread through both my son, and myself, was the greatest feeling. Isn't that what we were designed and created for? May your acts of kindness become less random.

Hebrews 13:2

"Be not forgetful to entertain strangers: for thereby some have entertained angels unawares."

CHAPTER 14 – FIVE MORE MINUTES

Joanne: "Come on little boy. It's time to go to bed."

Will: "How about five more minutes? What's five minutes in the grand scheme of things?"

Five more minutes. How often have we asked for just five more minutes? Five more minutes to delay bedtime, five more minutes to enjoy a spectacular sunset, five more minutes to avoid getting out of our comfy bed or five more minutes to tell a loved one goodbye. Only five more minutes…only three hundred seconds.

I recently read a book entitled "The 10 Second Rule: Following Jesus Made Simple" by Clare De Graaf. It has a simple directive. "Just do the next thing you're reasonably certain Jesus wants you to do – and do it within the next ten seconds." The premise is that we should not overthink or try to talk ourselves out of showing Christ-like behavior to those around us. Seems simple enough doesn't it? But how often are we so wrapped up in our lives to even notice those round us? Can we put our phones down long enough?

A few years ago, my son and I were on vacation in the northern part of the lower peninsula of Michigan, exploring Sleeping Bear Dunes. It is one of the most beautiful places in my gorgeous home state. The sand dunes stretch over fifty thousand miles and running down those dunes is one of the most memorable experiences of my childhood. After a long day of exploring the dunes, my son and I stopped by a local Cracker Barrel for dinner. On the porch an old man sat in one of the white rocking chairs next to a checkers board. My son approached the gentleman and asked if he wanted to play a game of checkers with him. For the next forty-five minutes that man showed patience and kindness to a little boy, even sharing a few tips and tricks along the way. That experience is one of my favorite memories of that vacation. I feel that the giving of our time to someone else is one of the greatest gifts we can bestow. That gift is always the perfect size and never needs a gift receipt.

So how can we build simple acts of kindness into every day?

Did a stranger pass by me who really needed to see a warm smile? Did that drive-thru attendant need a kind word because the vehicle in front of me just berated her for messing up their order? Does that new mom at the grocery store need an extra hand because she is learning how to navigate a car seat and a full grocery cart for the first time? None of these (change to "these") examples need a higher education or a certificate of achievement. They just need our willingness to look around and see others and then act…within ten seconds. And maybe brush up on your checkers skills.

Proverbs 3:3

"Do not let kindness and truth leave you; Bind them around your neck, Write them on the tablet of your heart."

CHAPTER 15 – A NEW NORMAL

Will: "Mom, when Jesus comes back to make a new earth do, we get to keep our bodies?"

Joanne: "Well, I don't know. I do know that our bodies will never get hurt or sick though."

Will: "That's good! But I do not want to be a girl okay? I just want to stay a boy."

Earlier this summer my son tried out for a local club soccer team, a club that he has been playing with for the past three years. On the night of try-outs, he spent two hours displaying his soccer skills, confident that he had done well. A few days later I was notified that my son had not made the team he was hoping to join. He was offered a spot on another team and he reluctantly agreed to give it a shot. When you are ten years old, not being on the same team with familiar faces is a HUGE disappointment. A new coach, new players, new positions – a "new normal."

A new normal is described as "a current state of being after some dramatic change has transpired. What replaces the expected, usual, typical state after an event occurs. The new normal encourages one to deal with current situations rather than lamenting what could have been."

What is your new normal? Have you suffered the loss of a job or devastating health diagnosis? No matter what your new normal is, I bet that there is nothing normal about it. This week a very dear friend of mine will begin chemo treatments and that will be her new normal. My best friend will get her son fitted for leg braces as that has become her new normal. Another dear friend will start an early retirement after her job was eliminated and she will have to find her new normal.

When a new normal season of life hits, doesn't it feel like you are powerless? No matter how hard you try, everything is out of your control? During those seasons I just want to hide under my covers like I did when I was a kid when a powerful thunderstorm thrashed outside my window. Unfortunately hiding under the covers is not as convenient when we are adults, but we still have power at our fingertips. We can clasp our fingers together, bend our knees, and ask for our Heavenly Father's assurance to see us through our new normal.

How else can we avoid feeling powerless? We can lament about what could or should have been, why it is not fair, and why did it have to happen to us. I truly believe that giving ourselves the time to grieve through those steps is very important. However, we cannot stay there. We need to press forward. The power lies in the moment we make a simple choice. We must choose between being bitter or getting better. We must acknowledge that this new season is going to hurt, that it most likely will leave scars (some visible and others not), and we will not be the same person prior to this season; but it will not destroy us. Maybe we need to say that repeatedly, but it works. It was the phrase I said to myself every time I faced a failed relationship, a job loss, and my divorce. This will NOT destroy me.

No matter how long or short your new normal season is, I pray that you claim the power you have within you, starting with a prayer to the One who knitted you together in your mother's womb. He will cover you through the darkest of nights and the longest of days. He knows you cannot face this new normal season alone and He does not expect you to. He longs to hear your voice and offer you reassurance that **"neither death nor life, neither angels nor demons, neither the present, nor the future, nor any powers, neither height nor depth, nor anything else in all creation, will be able to separate us from the love of God that is in Christ Jesus our Lord." Romans 8:38-19**

Isaiah 43: 18-19

"Forget the former things; do not dwell on the past. See, I am doing a new thing! Now it springs up; do you not perceive it? I am making a way in the wilderness and streams in the wasteland."

CHAPTER 16 – PARTY TIME

Joanne: "Do you remember when I told you that sometimes people get germs that make their bodies stop working?

Will: "Yeah, so then they die and go to heaven and have a party?"

Joanne: "Yes, that's right. Well, Grandma has those germs, buddy."

Will: "Is Grandma going to go to heaven and have a party without us?"

Joanne: "She is just going to go to heaven and get the party ready."

Will: "Mom, is Grandma your mom like you are my mom?"

Joanne: "Yes, that's right."

Will: "Someday are you going to go to heaven and have a party without me?"

"She has three months." That is what the oncologist said as I sat in his office on a beautiful spring day. As I gathered my courage, I looked across the room at my mother and tears were streaming down her face. "Do you have cancer Joanne?" she asked with a confused look on her face. "No, mom" was all I could whisper. My mother's mind and body had already been crippled with the deteriorating effects of Parkinson's for the past 8 years, and now that scary word, CANCER, had reared its ugly head. It was a fight that she could not and would not win. Three months would be all that we had to spend with her before she would be called home. As I left the office, I spent my entire drive back home trying to come up with something I could say to my six-year-old son.

How do you explain death and the loss of a beloved grandmother to a little boy? A grandmother who waited anxiously at the hospital during an emergency C-section and held him the night he was born. A grandmother who visited him every Friday during my maternity leave just so she could nap with him. A grandmother who always had a cookie to share and unlimited hugs and kisses to give. A grandmother who bragged to anyone within hearing distance all about her grandchildren; a job she was over-qualified for and should have had decades to enjoy.

What would I say to my son? How would I explain that death is a part of living and that everyone will feel the loss of a loved one? The sorrow of that loss will stay with us long after their smell has faded from their favorite shirt, their chair at the table is filled, and the tears fall less frequently.

Death feels so final because that loved one is no longer around for us to hug or create memories with. Is that why we refer to funerals as memorial services? Or should they be a celebration of life? I love that idea…a celebration. During our lives, we have celebrations for lots of reasons. The birth of a child, baptism, holidays, birthdays, weddings, and anniversaries. We take pictures and share those memories because celebrations make us happy. So, when a loved one's earthly life is done and they are called to their eternal home, shouldn't that be a cause for celebration? Their new home is a place where they will spend their days praising their Creator, free from burdens, free from bodies that fail, free from pain and loss. It is a place that rejoices in a lost sheep that is found, a prodigal son that returns, and a soul that has come home. I am confident that they will throw a party: a party filled with tears of joy and cookies.

2 Corinthians 5:1-2

"For we know that when this earthly tent we live in is taken down (that is, when we die and leave this earthly body), we will have a house in heaven, an eternal body made for us by God himself and not by human hands. We

grow weary in our present bodies, and we long to put on our heavenly bodies like new clothing."

CHAPTER 17 – A TIME TO DANCE

Will: "What does it mean to get married?"

Joanne: "What do you think it means?"

Will: "I think it means you take a LOT of pictures".

Joanne: "Yes, that's true."

Will: "And then there's some dancing".

Joanne: "Yes, that too".

Will: "Are you going to get married?"

Joanne "I don't know."

Will: "Well, don't worry about the dancing because I will dance with you".

There it was. One of the questions I had dreaded being asked ever since I had become divorced and joined the ranks of single mothers. "What does it mean to get married?" My 6-year-old son had just returned from Hawaii where he participated in his father's second wedding and his curiosity was piqued. For any of you that have a curious child, you know they cannot be pacified with a simple 'yes' or 'no' answer, and that the questions will not stop until you satisfied their need for understanding. Today's curiosity was about getting married. How hard could that be?

Getting married: what an exciting time in life! From the moment of your engagement to the reception, and every cake tasting, seating chart and bridal shower in between, the entire process is a thrilling adventure. "I do" seems like the simplest two words to say and "happily ever after" is what you will be.

Then one day, you are not happy, and those words are replaced with "I do not love you anymore and I am serving you with divorce papers." No Hallmark card can even come close to expressing the words you want to hear and no registry gift from Bed, Bath and Beyond will be arriving on your doorstep. Couples dinners will be replaced with third wheel sympathy dinners and your non-parenting weekends will be filled with frozen waffles and hours of ER reruns. Hey, no judgement here because I have been there.

I know what the Bible teaches about love. "Love is patient, love is kind. It does not envy, it does not boast, it is not proud. It does not dishonor others, it is not self-seeking, it is not easily angered, and it keeps no record of wrongs. Love never fails." Prior to joining the divorced club, I had believed all those things. Divorce seems like a failure of love to me. Vows were spoken, promises were made and then broken. What could I tell my son about marriage, love, and happily ever? In my opinion, happily ever after belongs only in fairy tales. Or those romantic comedies, usually starring Reese Witherspoon with a cute leading man, are the stuff of movie magic.

So, what advice can I give my son about marriage? I told him that it takes work, LOTS of work, and sometimes hurtful words are said. Promises might be broken and vows could be forgotten. Sometimes a person can walk away but that is not the end of the story. I am hopeful that there will more opportunities to love, to take pictures and to dance. Even if my dancing partner needs to stand on my feet.

1 Corinthians 13:4-7

"Love is patient, love is kind. It does not envy, it does not boast, it is not proud. It does not dishonor others, it is not self-seeking, it is not easily angered, it keeps no record of wrongs. Love does not delight in evil but rejoices with the truth. It always protects, always trusts, always hopes, always perseveres."

CHAPTER 18 – REST ASSURED

Will "Hey mom, I'm just a little tired; not big tired, okay?"

Blah. That is my word for the day. Today my level of productivity is about 2%. I have got dishes piled in the sink, laundry that needs folding and a list of other projects that I would like to tackle but all of those are going to be ignored. I have had pajamas on since mid-afternoon and I am looking forward to a night of rest and relaxation. Meriam Webster defines rest as "a bodily state characterized by minimal functional and metabolic activities". That is exactly what I am doing today…just the bare minimum. Rest is also defined as "peace of mind or spirit." That is something I long for.

I like making lists. I love to make lists of vacations that I would like to take and places I would like to visit. I make lists of home projects I would like to complete. I make lists of gifts I want to purchase for loved ones. I make grocery lists and lists of menus for the week ahead. I even make a list of accomplishments I have completed just so I can remind myself of how productive I have been. Perhaps I need to take a rest from making lists. Of all the lists that I have ever made I am 100% sure that I never put the word "rest" on a list. Not sleep or meditative stillness but rest, a peace of mind or spirit.

From the beginning of time, we are told that God, who had just spoken creation into existence, decided that creating a day for rest, was His very next task. Was God tired? Or did He just need time to unwind and enjoy the fruits of His labor? He certainly would have reason to be basking in the glow of all that He had accomplished. Creating the heavens, the earth, light, and darkness are no small endeavors. Lighting up the skies with the moon, the sun and all the stars. From ladybugs to elephants and every creature in-between God gave each creature the breath of life. And if those accomplishments were not enough, He created man, from the deepest part of His heart. Then God took the time to bless His work and chose one day to be reserved for rest. I like the sound of that. Blessing my work from the past week and then resting.

Genesis 2:2-3 "And on the seventh day God finished his work that he had done, and he rested on the seventh day from all his work that he had done. So, God blessed the seventh day and

made it holy, because God rested from all his work that he had done in creation."

Resting is not something that comes easily to me. How about you? I feel that I must "earn" a time to rest. Only after I have had a long week of work can I sit down to enjoy a movie. Or I push myself too much, while neglecting my personal health, until illness or utter fatigue force me to take a break. The Bible provides warning to us about spreading ourselves too thin.

"It is in vain that you rise up early and go late to rest, eating the bread of anxious toil; for He gives to his beloved sleep." Psalm 127:2

What kind of rest should we try to obtain? Is the recommended eight hours of sleep the only type of rest we should seek? A good night's sleep will restore our physical body but how do we provide rest to our emotional and mental selves?

"I lay down and slept; I woke again, for the Lord sustained me." Psalm 3:5

For our emotional rest I think we need to look at what causes our emotional UN-rest. Are we anxious? Worried? Are we passing judgement of others based solely on what is being splashed over social media? What would happen if we took a rest from negative thoughts and words? What if we made the choice NOT to comment on every post that we did not agree with and just kept scrolling?

"Besides, they get into the habit of being idle and going about from house to house. And not only do they become idlers but also gossips and busybodies, saying things they ought not to." 1 Timothy 5:13

Then there is mental health. In my opinion mental health is such a crucial aspect of our existence. Even as my son adjusts to virtual education due to the COVID-19 crisis his teacher is sending out mental health check-in reports so that the students can communicate their feelings. Are they happy, sad, angry, or frustrated? I think I might have to borrow that report. After a full day of school tutoring, working, household chores and making sure we get more exercise than screen time I bet I could put a check mark in every one of those categories! So how do we give rest to our mental selves?

"You keep him in perfect peace whose mind is stayed on you, because he trusts in you." Isaiah 26:3

So perhaps the secret to finding true rest is keeping our hearts, minds and souls focused on the One who can provide everything that we need. He is just a prayer away and visiting with Him does not require a face mask, hand sanitizer or social distancing.

Luke 10:27 "He answered, "'Love the Lord your God with all your heart and with all your soul and with all your strength and with all your mind'; and 'Love your neighbor as yourself.'"

CHAPTER 19 – DIRTY DISHES

Will: "Did you know there is nothing to do in the Principal's office? I mean nothing! First you have to sit and then you have to talk."

Mom: "What were you doing in the Principal's office?"

Will: "Well my fist accidentally hit someone."

Do you know the best time to visit the Principals' office? Never! But do you know the most convenient time for a dishwasher to stop working? The night before you are hosting a dinner party. But I am getting ahead of myself. Let us go back a few weeks to where the idea for this dinner party first began. One day I was busy cleaning out my freezer, one of those exciting jobs you do as an adult and noticed that I had a rather large pork tenderloin taking up premium freezer space. I knew my ten-year-old son would much rather enjoy his usual diet of hot dogs, mac and cheese and chicken fingers over pork tenderloin so who else could I share this with?

A few nights later I was busy organizing my pantry and I came across the twelve-piece serving set of china I had received as a wedding present from a marriage that had ended nine years ago. Why had I hung onto this? Most of the time my son and I use paper plates and paper towels for dinner, and I could count on one hand the number of times I had used the china set in the past ten years. When was the next time I would need this?

That evening I took my dog for a walk around my small condo subdivision and I sporadically stopped to chat with neighbors who were sitting on their porches. I am convinced that a dog is the best way to meet your neighbors. Even though I am an extrovert by nature starting conversations with strangers is not as comfortable for me as it would seem. Over the past few years, I have gotten to know about a dozen neighbors who live by themselves due to divorce, the death of a spouse or other tough situations. While each situation is unique, we face some of the same struggles. How do you cook for one person? How do you make new friends when your spouse has died, or you experienced a divorce or perhaps you have never been married? By the end of my walk, I knew what I was being called to do. It was time to dust of those fancy dishes, defrost that pork tenderloin and have a dinner party.

Lucky for me I have a few neighbors who have been in my condo subdivision longer than I have so they graciously offered to help me pass out invitations and put together a tasty menu. Between the three of us we passed out a dozen invitations and as the dinner date approached, I received several phone calls from guests who were excited to RSVP and could not wait to attend!

The night before the dinner party I loaded my dishwasher and pushed the start button. Nothing happened. I pushed the start button again. Nothing happened. As panic started to set in, I proceeded to push every single button on my dishwasher's panel and lights flashed but nothing happened. I anxiously googled ideas on trouble-shooting dishwashers, I reset the breaker and I prayed. I could not welcome first-time guests into my home with a sink full of dirty dishes. What would they think?

Finally, the dinner day and time arrived and several of my guests arrived early, so excited to step outside their doors, and comfort zones, to share a meal together. For the next three hours eight lovely ladies shared a meal and so much more. It is amazing what can happen when you surround your table with neighbors.

In Jen Hatmaker's new book entitled "For the Love" she captures this shared table concept so simply. "...maybe just invite some folks over. A shared table is the supreme expression of hospitality in every culture on earth. When your worn-out kitchen table hosts good people and good conversations, when it provides a safe place to break bread and good wine your house becomes a sanctuary, holy as a cathedral."

I do not know if my sink full of dirty dishes could be compared to a sanctuary, but I am certain that sharing a meal is the perfect opportunity to love on my neighbors. And wouldn't you know it? My dishwasher started right up as soon as the dishes were cleared from the table.

Deuteronomy 12:7

"And there you shall eat before the Lord your God, and you shall rejoice, you and your households, in all that you undertake, in which the Lord your God has blessed you.

CHAPTER 20 – RUN AND NOT GROW WEARY

Joanne "Hey buddy guess what? This weekend we are going to an indoor water park. There will be go-karts, water slides, and lots of other fun things.

Will "Do I have to miss my soccer game?"

Joanne "Yes, but just this one game."

Will "Mom if I ever have to choose between soccer and anything else, I'm going to choose soccer."

My son always seems to be running. Why walk when you can run…across the living room, down the stairs and out the door. Everywhere and anywhere his body desires to go you can bet it is with great speed. Even in his sleep his legs are constantly moving. So, it was no surprise that when I introduced him to organized soccer, at the age of five, he took to it like a fish to water. Chasing a ball up and down a field appears to be his current passion. Whether it is ninety-four degrees out with 100% humidity, snowing with temperatures right above the freezing mark or my personal favorite, the side-ways rain that no umbrella can hold up against, he loves that sport. And I love that he has a passion for it. What are you passionate about? What makes you so happy that simply walking is not an option? What would get you off the couch and running?

One evening I threw a going away party for some amazing friends who were relocating to Las Vegas. These amazing friends were the kind of neighbors whose house you knew like your own, where dinner was always shared and where you could walk in without knocking. Our boys were the best of friends and every other week a slumber party was hosted. Not only was my son going to miss his best friend, but I was going to miss mine. As with any highly emotional event toasts were made, tears were shed, and memories captured and posted to social media. It was the perfect evening.

The next morning, I awoke to several text messages about where to purchase running shoes, training plans and encouragement about my decision. What decision had I made during an emotional farewell? That perfect evening had apparently taken a wrong turn at some point and I was a bit hazy on where and when. Then it hit me. When sharing a table with experienced long-distance runners limit your drink intake! Apparently, I had carelessly committed to running a ½ marathon in Las Vegas in a few short months. The only problem was that I was not a runner. NOT a long-distance runner by any means and the only short distance running I was currently doing was running my son to school, soccer practice and the grocery store. These days I was practicing a more relaxed, yet intensive workout regimen of yoga which involved dimmed lights, controlled breathing, and no fancy footwear. But I had given my word and there were witnesses who were going to hold me accountable.

So, my running journey began as any other journey does, with one foot in front of the other. I visited a local footwear store and purchased my fitted shoes for my flat feet and weak ankles. I upgraded my current work-out wardrobe of ratty tank tops and yoga pants with color-coordinated running attire and matching water bottle. I looked the part of a runner, but the hard part had not even started yet. I printed off the running training schedule and posted it on the refrigerator so it was a visual reminder that could not be ignored. All that was left to do was to start running. I did not think about how far and utterly impossible 13.1 miles seemed or the fact that my body had not run in over 10 years. I did not think about how far-fetched the idea was that I expected my forty-one-year-old body to move with grace and fluidity given its long hiatus. I inhaled, exhaled, and focused on running that first mile. One mile, that was all I needed to do. I will be completely honest here in that I have no idea how long it took me to run that mile or if you could even call it "running" but I got it done. Then that one mile turned into two, then three and so on. Over the course of the next three months, I laced up my running shoes day after day and conquered mile after mile until I reached my goal. Then, on a clear and crisp night, I crossed the finish line of a 13.1 half marathon down the famous Las Vegas strip and a finishers medal was hung around my neck. I know that someday when I cross that final finish line that I can look back and see that I ran every race with endurance; even those races that seemed impossible and insurmountable. That the One hanging the medal around my neck will say "well done good and faithful servant".

Isaiah:40-31

"But those who hope in the LORD will renew their strength. They will soar on wings like eagles; they will run and not grow weary; they will walk and not be faint."

CHAPTER 21 – MAYBE SHE'S BORN WITH IT?

Will "Mom I'm pretty sure you are like a genius."

Joanne "Well where do you think you get those smarty pants from?"

Will "God"

In 1991, the "Maybe she's born with it. Maybe it's Maybelline" advertising slogan was introduced and became one of the most recognizable slogans around the world. Since Maybelline is a cosmetic company, I am sure their slogan has more to do with clear skin, perfectly blended blush and a flawless smokey eye but very few "real" women I know are born with those attributes. I have always been grateful that I inherited blue eyes, dark hair and, up until I reached 40, a fast metabolism. These days my blue eyes need reading glasses, my dark hair needs coloring touch-ups, and that metabolism has left the building. However, I know without a doubt that I have something more valuable and crucial to my beauty regime than any item I can find in the local HBC aisle. Grit. Grit is defined as "courage and resolve; strength of character." I do not know if a person is born with grit or if it develops as they experience life. What do you think?

I have seen life deal out some heavy blows to loved ones, strangers on the news and even myself. Life altering blows that brought even the strongest believers to their knees and shattered their hopes and dreams. Who could blame them if they just gave up, or got so consumed by their grief that they were just a shell of the person they once were? But what gets that person out of bed when everything around them seems hopeless?

Are you familiar with the story of Job in the Old Testament? Job was just going along in life, enjoying the fruits of his labor, when tragedy upon tragedy began to befall him. First, he lost his livestock, then his servants and then all his offspring. **Job 1:20-22 says "When Job heard this, he tore his clothes and shaved his head because of his great sorrow. He knelt on the ground, then worshiped God and said: "We bring nothing at birth; we take nothing with us at death. The Lord alone gives and takes.**

Praise the name of the Lord!" Despite everything, Job did not sin or accuse God of doing wrong.

I do not know about you, but I cannot even begin to comprehend the level of Job's grief. Grief so powerful that it required a physical reaction of shaving one's head and tearing one's clothing. I would more likely want to scream, punch something or throw something just to hear it smash. Yet, Job has enough grit to make a choice, amid his grief, to kneel and worship God. Not only worship God but acknowledge that everything is God's and He alone can take and give as He desires. That is some grit! I wonder if Job had experienced earlier lessons in life that allowed him to mature his threshold of grit to such an inspiring level.

A few nights ago, my son was at soccer practice and during a scrimmage he took a ball right in his face. Thankfully, he was spared a bloody nose but the sting of the ball against his face quickly brought tears to his eyes and he went over to the sidelines to take a break. A few minutes later I saw that he had wiped his face, walked back on the field, and resumed his position. In years prior he would have given up and insisted on sitting out the rest of practice; no matter how much prompting his mother or coach gave him. Something inside of his little body convinced him that a ball to the face was not worth missing out on the thrill of the game. In my opinion, that is how grit starts. It starts with something small where we have a choice to make. A choice to make on whether to give up or not and every time we wipe our tears away and get back in the game, we are choosing grit over surrender. My hope and prayer to you, my friend, is that you GRIT UP every opportunity you get.

Romans 2:7

"To those who by persistence in doing good seek glory, honor and immortality, he will give eternal life."

CHAPTER 22 – AVOID BIG FISH

Will: "Mom, third grade isn't all sunshine and rainbows."

Joanne: "Neither is being a grown-up, pal."

Have you ever clicked an email, quickly glanced over the contents, and then instantly regretted opening the message to begin with? Maybe you can just mark it as unread so that the sender cannot see that you have received and read it? Or you could ignore it and pretend like you never got it. Of course, it is highly unlikely your conscience will be able to gloss over that, but it might be worth it for a little while. Who really wants to live a 100% guilt-free life anyway? Where is the fun in that?

This email was not spam or someone asking for money. It did not contain insults, complaints, or an impossible demand. Quite the opposite. in fact. It contained one simple request so why was this such a big deal? The sender wanted to visit the church that I attend. Simple enough. I just needed to type a quick response, try not to overthink it. and move on with my day. The request was not the problem. I was more concerned with the sender of the email.

Do you remember the Bible story about Jonah? He was an Old Testament character who was a prophet. A prophet was someone who proclaimed the will of God. If you needed repentance, a prophet would let you know. Jonah and God were supposed to be on the same page and probably had one of those complicated handshakes. God had given Jonah a simple directive and Jonah responded like any rational, mature adult would. He ran away…in the opposite direction. When it comes to difficult decisions, we all have that fight or flight instinct. That is exactly what I wanted to do when I read that email: hide, run away, or feign ignorance. I did not choose one of those options because I was afraid of getting swallowed by a big fish. That is exactly what happened to

Jonah and I knew God was not going to let me off the hook if I simply chose to ignore His directive.

Ever since I became a single, divorced, mom walking into church and having to sit by myself has been one of the most challenging things I have had to do. I can easily dine alone, attend a movie by myself, and have mastered the art of traveling solo but sitting alone at church has been one area that I have continually struggled with. For years I have prayed for someone to sit next to, besides my little boy, so that I would not feel so out of place. So here was God offering me an answer to that prayer via email. How much more direct can God be? However, it was not the answer to my pray that I had imagined in my head. Instead, it someone who had the courage to reach out, knowing how awkward the situation might be, yet willing to take the risk. In a moment of courage and obedience I responded to the email. A few weeks later, I attended church and was joined by my son and his stepmother. My emailed response had been received. Was this God's answer to my prayer, a test of faith to not just talk the talk but walk the walk, or both? During the service we sat together, sang together, and prayed together. The smile on my son's face was radiant. He sat between two women who loved him, who were making the best of a situation, and who were willing to sit together in a situation that was uncomfortable and awkward, with no big fish in sight.

2 John 1:6

"And this is love: that we walk in obedience to his commands. As you have heard from the beginning, his command is that you walk in love."

CHAPTER 23 - SCARS

Will: "Mom I'm probably a little grouchy today and I am not sure how long it will last."

Do you have any scars? I grew up on a farm as a bit of a tomboy, with two older brothers that I tried to keep up with, and a younger sister that tagged along. I wanted to be right in the thick of the action and that curiosity earned me several trips to the small-town urgent care facility. In fact, I was on first name basis with the ER team due to the frequency of my visits. I earned myself sprained ankles, a broken arm, and multiple stitches. I have two scars as a result and over the years the scars have faded but they will remain with me for as long as I have this earthly body. They no longer hurt but I can remember the pain that I experienced when I got them. I remember feeling embarrassed by their visibility and wishing that I had not been so careless.

What about the scars we cannot see? How deep do they run, and do they ever heal? Do they fade with the passage of time? Do they impact our daily lives, even though they cannot be seen by others? Some emotional scars are surface deep and with time they will fade away. Other scars are very deep and there is no amount of time that will heal them. They are jagged and ugly. Sometimes you do not know they exist until someone mentions a word or phrase, and that unknown scar throbs like the lightning bolt on Harry Potter's forehead.

A few weeks ago, I had the pleasure of heading to one of my favorite beaches with two dear friends. They are the type of friends that conversations containing both humor and authenticity flow deep and wide. During our visit, one of my friends mentioned that she knew how much I had wanted more children but how that just was not part of my reality. It takes a courageous friend to speak about your disappointment even though you do not remember mentioning it before. Before I knew it, tears were steaming down my face and I was surrounded with warm hugs. I had no idea that scar even existed or how much of an emotional reaction it would create.

Recently, another scar that was brought to my attention was bitterness. That sure is an ugly word. What exactly is bitterness? Psychologist and blogger, Stephen Diamond, Ph.D. defines bitterness as "a chronic and pervasive state of smoldering resentment," and regards it as "one of the most destructive and toxic of human emotions." Yikes! I doubt anyone wants to be described as a bitter person but all too often our hurts and disappointments, if ignored or left to fester too long, will turn into bitterness. A bitter person tends to jealous, holds grudges, and cannot express genuine happiness for other people. Sounds like an awful way to live.

I can remember a time when my emotional scars began to shift into a season of bitterness. If someone celebrated a wedding anniversary, I could not congratulate them because I was divorced, and anniversaries were painful dates on the calendar that I struggled to get through. If I received a wedding invitation, I would either throw it in the trash or give some lame excuse as to why I could not (or would not) attend. If a friend were enjoying the blissful phase of a new relationship, I would listen and smile while they shared their happiness, but inwardly I seethed with jealousy.

How does one survive that type of season, and most importantly, not get stuck there? As far as I know, there is no magic pill, or a self-help book on rooting out bitterness. It takes hard work. The kind of emotional work that is not completed in one therapy session or a heart to heart with a close friend. Once bitterness is planted, its roots began to spread, choking out the joy and happiness in our lives until our words become harsh and our behavior is hurtful. If we are not careful, even our health will suffer. Bitterness feeds on the unfairness that we see or interpret in our lives, and that is no way to live.

These days I can celebrate my friends' anniversaries with a sincere congratulation, attend weddings with a joyful heart and smile, inside and out, as a friend shares the excitement of a new relationship. It is not because I am married, getting married or in any kind of special relationship. It is because my heart has let go of the bitterness. It took lots of prayers (mine and others for me), forgiveness of myself for mistakes I have made, and the telling of my story. My unique, beautiful, messy story. I bet you have one too, and likely a few scars to boot. Those are my favorite kind of people – even when they are grouchy.

Ephesians 4: 31-23

"Let all bitterness and wrath and anger and clamor and slander be put away from you, along with all malice. Be kind to one another, tender-hearted, forgiving each other, just as God in Christ also has forgiven you."

CHAPTER 24 – WE ARE RICH!

Will: "Mom, how much money do we have?"

Joanne: "We have just enough and a little extra."

Will: "So we are rich then?"

Joanne: "You think we are rich?"

Will: "We have everything we need."

Joanne: "Then we are rich beyond measure, little boy."

"Your position has been eliminated." Odds are that at some point in life most of us have heard or will hear that phrase. Perhaps the company is down-sizing, being acquired or merging with another company. Either way that means you are on the cutting block and will join the ranks of the unemployed. For me that was the end of a position that I loved and a company that I respected. I had spent the last five years, trying to keep managers within their budgets, getting financials done in a timely fashion and teaching others the tricks of Microsoft Excel. Did you know that a spreadsheet has ties to Star Wars? R2 and D2. See, us accountant types can be funny too. I knew at seventeen that I wanted to be an accountant. I went to business school, earned my degree, and have enjoyed what I do every day since. I love numbers, love spreadsheets, and even spend my spare time helping others with personal budgeting. By the way I know how geeky that makes me sound and I am 100% okay with that. If we look deep enough, we all have a geeky side. Yes, even you.

I wanted to be an accountant because I never wanted money to control me. I never wanted it to be a taboo subject or the cause of arguments and strained relationships. I figured that if I understood how to manage it, it could not manage me. I have put money into my retirement account, built up a savings and have given my tithes diligently. It was all managed so well and carefully. Then I became an unemployed single parent, and my financial security took a beating. My carefully managed spreadsheet had a lot more negative numbers, and I was afraid. There was not a second income from a spouse to help me. I was drowning with divorce attorney fees and therapy bills, and a little boy who did not need to know about my financial fears. But eventually even the strongest will break when the weight becomes too much to bear.

After I tucked my son into bed one night, I collapsed on the floor of my room; overcome with sadness, anger, and fear. I was devastated over the demise of my marriage, angry with the responsibility of having to manage life on my own and fear of the unknown. My prayers of anguish and sorrow went on for hours. I cried and cried and cried. How was I going to keep this ship afloat when even my life raft was sinking? I lashed out at the only person that I knew was listening…my God. How could all of this be happening? When will it end? Why have you allowed this?

Several hours into my emotional breakdown I heard the faintest whisper of a voice with a very direct message. "Walk away from your job and I will take care of you". "Well, that's it" I thought. "I'm hearing voices so I'm definitely experiencing a mental breakdown along with an emotional one." This voice did not sound mean or direct me to hurt myself or others. However, it was asking me to give up the only thing that was holding my ramshackle life together. My position had been eliminated a few months prior and I had quickly found another place of employment, but it was not a good fit. It made me miserable and I was not giving myself or my employer my best. But who cares about that when you are a single parent, and it is a sizable paycheck?

Then I heard that whisper again. "Walk away from your job and I will take care of you." It is strange enough to argue with yourself when making life decisions but arguing with someone who is only issuing one directive and barely above a whisper is something else entirely. Give up the one thing I had left? Stop going to work? Stop living my life eight to five, analyzing spreadsheets, balancing checkbooks, and recording journal entries? And do what? At the age of eighteen, I moved out of my parent's home, went to college, worked multiple jobs simultaneously so I could afford my apartment and pay my tuition. The only time I was not working was during my eight-week maternity leave, but then I had guaranteed employment when I returned. Now, I was being instructed to quit my job and have no plan? What sense does that make? None, I tell you, but then neither does life sometimes. I finally concluded that having no plan is sometimes a smarter choice than having a bad plan, so I eventually closed my eyes and slept the most peaceful sleep I had experienced in years.

The next day I went to my office, cleaned out my desk and left a note under the human resources door that read "I resign effective immediately. I just want to play with my son." I went home, stopped wearing my watch, took a break from social media and experienced life through the eyes of a 3-year-old.

What a rejuvenating time that was! We explored every neighborhood park, played trains, laughed at stories involving a silly little monkey named George, took naps, and blew bubbles in our backyard. That glorious "plan" continued for 8 weeks and it will forever be etched into my memory as the most fulfilled time of my life. A few weeks into that break, I was tucking my son into bed for the night. His checks were sun-kissed from a day at the beach and he smelled like summer. Then my son confidentially stated, "Mom and Will are happy." I do not know the true cost of happiness, but I can bet it is a lot less than most of us realize. After those eight weeks were finished, a job opportunity came my way that allowed me to work four days a week and gave me the perfect life and work balance. It is amazing how that quiet voice knew what I needed right when I needed it. All I needed to do was to let go of my plan.

1 Kings 19: 11-13

"And, behold, the Lord passed by, and a great and strong wind shook the mountains, and broke in pieces the rocks before the Lord; but the Lord was not in the wind. After the wind an earthquake, but the Lord was not in the earthquake. And after the earthquake a fire; but the Lord was not in the fire. And after the fire came a still small voice…"

Photography Credit – Jennifer Marie Photography

Made in the USA
Monee, IL
22 February 2021